RIGHT TO INFORMATION ACT 2005

A PRIMER

Popular Social Science

National Campaign for Peoples Right to Information

RIGHT TO INFORMATION ACT 2005

A PRIMER

SUCHI PANDE
SHEKHAR SINGH

National Book Trust, India

ISBN 978-81-237-5075-0

First Edition 2007
First Reprint 2008
Second Reprint 2009 (Saka 1930)

Rs. 30.00

Published by the Director, National Book Trust, India
Nehru Bhawan, 5 Institutional Area, Phase-II
Vasant Kunj, New Delhi-110070

Dedicated
to the memory of
journalist and RTI Campaigner
late Prakash Kardaley
Member of Working Committee of the NCPRI,
founder of 'Hum Janenge'

Contents

Acknowledgements

This primer draws heavily on the primers made earlier by Parivartan and NCPRI, and various other documents too numerous to list here. We also gratefully acknowledge the website of the Commonwealth Human Rights Initiative (CHRI) as a valuable source of information. Information was also collected from the websites of the Central Information Commission, The Government of India and various State Governments and Information Commissions.

We also gratefully acknowledge the very useful comments given by various participants of the Training of Trainers workshop organized by the Consumer and Legal Help Society, at Sawai Madhopur, Rajasthan on 19&20 November 2006 and the Mazdoor Kisan Shakti Sangathan (MKSS) on 26 December 2006.

The authors are grateful to Aruna Roy, Nikhil Dey, Arvind Kejriwal, Manish Sisodia, Anjali Bhardwaj, Angela Rangad, Tarun Bhartiya and the Working Committee of the NCPRI for useful suggestions.

July 2007 — Suchi Pande
New Delhi — Shekhar Singh

Introduction

Do you wonder ...

- **What you can do about the ration shop in your village/town/area that never has any ration?**
- **What you can do if your local panchayat or municipality does so little and always claims that they have no funds?**
- **What you can do if there is no doctor, or no medicines, at the primary health center/hospital and no health worker at the sub-health center/ dispensary?**
- **What you can do to get your rights without having to pay a bribe?**
- **What you can do if the schoolteacher is always absent?**
- **What you can do if the streets and colonies in your town/city are dirty?**
- **What you can do if the roads in your area are in a pathetic condition?**
- **What you can do to ensure that people do not die of starvation in various parts of the country?**

- **Why, when so much money is supposedly being spent on our welfare, there are still so many people who live in abject poverty?**

Some of us feel that this country would be a better place to live in if we had better politicians and bureaucrats. However, real change can come only when the people of this country hold their government and public servants accountable, so that they are forced to respond to the poorest citizen of this land. And when that happens, no public servant or government would dare to be corrupt, inefficient or insensitive.

But how do we hold the government and other public authorities accountable?

We cannot even begin to make the government and other public authorities accountable if we do not have the basic information regarding their decisions and functioning. The Right to Information Act that came into force on 12 October 2005, empowers us to do just that.

It gives us the right to question our public authorities and get information about matters that affect us in thousands of ways. Used innovatively, such information can make our government and other public authorities accountable to the people.

> We all pay taxes. Even the homeless person living on the streets pays tax. When she buys anything, like a matchbox or a soap, she pays sales tax, excise duty or VAT, etc. Therefore, the money that the government has is our money.

"In a government of responsibility like ours where the agents of the public must be responsible for their conduct there can be but a few secrets. The people of this country have a right to know every public act, everything that is done in a public way by their public functionaries. They are entitled to know the particulars of every public transaction in all its bearings." Supreme Court in State of UP vs Raj Narain, 1975

How does the RTI Act help us?

RTI Act gives you the right to ask the government and other public authorities for information that can expose inaction, arbitrariness, corruption, and address grievances.

Do you have pending work with any department of the Government? Are they not doing your work and expecting or demanding a bribe? Did you file any grievance petition in a government department but they are simply not acting on it? Did you make any complaint against any official or against any wrong-doing and they are not acting on your complaint? You can use the Right to Information Act to know the status of your application. Sometimes, demanding the status forces them to act.

Under the RTI Act you can:

- Demand from the government, or other public authorities, most types of information.
- Demand photocopies of contracts, receipts, estimates, measurements of engineering works etc.
- Demand samples of material used in the construction of roads, drains, buildings etc.
- Demand to inspect documents or ongoing and completed works.
- Demand status of your requests or complaints.
- Demand an explanation from the government for their actions and inaction.

RTI query: Why was auditor transferred?

Official reply: Under political pressure

In response to a Right to Information query on why a special auditor from Nashik was transferred before he completed his term, the Cooperative, Marketing and Textile Department has stated that the decision was taken "under political pressure".

Going one step further, the detailed reply says that the transfer of special auditor AMM, probing charges of corruption in the functioning of a Cooperative Bank, was done on the insistence of a powerful politician who was also the bank's director. AMM had audited the bank's records and had pointed out serious lapses in the functioning of the bank and highlighted alleged corruption. The report also made serious note of the bank's inability to recover loans from certain individuals.

"In this transfer case, there were many requests made, both in writing and orally, by local representatives. Based on this the transfer was considered," states the reply, adding that the department is inundated by such requests everyday and is under pressure to oblige them.

Days after AMM was transferred, PBK filed a request under the RTI Act, asking the cooperatives department why AMM had been transferred barely a year after he was appointed in the district. PBK received four pages from the PIO, including departmental notings on the matter.

Ironically, the department had initially rejected the transfer request stating that since AMM had not completed his tenure, he could not be moved out of Nashik district

Getting your entitlement through RTI

MN is a 70 year old rickshaw puller, from Madhubani, Bihar. His family comes under the Below Poverty Line category and is entitled to benefit under the national housing scheme (Indira Awas Yojana). The village Panchayat held that MN's family is entitled to the benefits of the scheme but five years later he still had not received anything. Instead, he was asked to pay a bribe of Rs. 5,000. MN filed an RTI application. Within a week of filing the application MN received a cheque of Rs. 15,000 (first installment) under the Indira Awas Yojna.

I

Salient Features of the Right to Information Act 2005

Getting Started

By using the RTI act it is possible to ensure good governance and get our rights. All you have to do is:

1. Identify the information that you need. Decide on the questions you want to ask. These can be as simple or as complex as you like. Do you want copies of documents or samples of materials? Do you want to inspect documents or materials? Or do you just want answers to specific questions? The more you already know about the department and how it functions, the more effective your questions will be.
2. Identify, as closely as you can, which public authority (department of the government, public sector enterprise, NGO, private body etc.) has the information that you want.

- You can seek information from any public authority (including departments of the central or state government, from panchayati raj institutions, from courts of law, the Parliament and state legislatures, and from other organizations and institutions – including NGOs – that are established, constituted, owned, controlled or substantially financed, directly or indirectly, by the state or central government) (section 2(h)).

- You an also ask the concerned government department to access for you information from any private body that the government can access under any other law (2(f)).

3. Find the contact details of the Public Information Officer for the public authority in question.

- In each public authority, one or more officers are required to be designated as public information officers (PIOs). They accept the requests for information and provide information sought by the people (5(1)).
- In addition, in each sub-district level there are required to be assistant public information officers (APIOs) who receive requests for information and appeals against decisions of the public information officers, and then send them to the appropriate public authorities (5(2)). The central government has designated various post offices across the country as APIOs where a citizen can deposit an RTI request or appeal pertaining to any central government public authority.

4. Write out your questions on a sheet of plain paper (For sample applications see Annexure 1).

- Any person seeking information should file an application on plain paper (or in the suggested format) with the public information officer/assistant public information officers (6(1)).
- Where a request cannot be made in writing, the PIO is obligated to render all reasonable assistance to the person making the request orally to reduce the same in writing (6(1)(b)).
- Where the applicant is sensorily challenged, the public authority is obligated to provide assistance to enable access to the information, including providing such assistance as may be appropriate for the inspection (7(4)).
- The applicant is not required to either give any reasons for requesting the information or any personal details, except those required to contact the applicant (6(2)).

5. Submit your application with your application fees, if required, to the PIO. Different states have different application fees, but by law all below-poverty-line (BPL) families are exempt from paying any fee. (For a copy of the Central Government rules see Annexure 2.) Don't forget to get a dated and stamped receipt for your RTI application, as well as a dated receipt for your payment, where a fee is paid!

- A reasonable application fee, as prescribed, will be charged for each application and for supply of information (for the fee prescribed please consult the fee rules for your state or for the central government, Parliament, Supreme Court, High Courts or state legislatures). However, no fee is chargeable from persons below the poverty line (7(5)), or if the information is provided after the prescribed period (7(6)).

6. You should get the information asked for within the prescribed period – usually 30 days.

- Information sought from the PIO has ordinarily to be provided or refused within 30 days. Information regarding the life or liberty of an individual has to be provided within 48 hours (7(1)). That sought from an APIO in 35 days (5(2)), and 40 days where third party information is involved (11(3)).

7. If you don't get your information within the prescribed time, or if you're dissatisfied with the information supplied, or with the reasons given for denying you information, file a first appeal, within 30 days, with the designated appellate authority in the public authority from which you have sought information (19(1)).
8. If you are dissatisfied with the response on the first appeal or if you do not get a response within 45 days of filing your first appeal, file a second appeal, within 90 days of the expiry of the 45 day

period, with the state information commission of the state to which the public authority belongs, or to the central information commission for central government public authorities (19(3)). (For addresses of chief information commissioners see Annexure 4)

9. You can also separately file a complaint (18(1)) with the state or central information commission, as applicable, if the PIO or APIO:

- Refuses to accept your application,
- Delays beyond the prescribed time period the provision of information,
- In your opinion malafidely denies you information,
- In your opinion knowingly gives incorrect, incomplete or misleading information or,
- In your opinion has knowingly destroyed information which was the subject of the request or obstructed in any manner in furnishing the information.

10. If your complaint is found correct by the concerned information commission, the relevant PIO/ APIO would be fined up to Rs. 25,000 and even departmental action can be initiated against him/ her.

- If a PIO fails to furnish the information asked for or fails to communicate the rejection order, within the time specified and without reasonable cause, the PIO shall be liable to pay a penalty of Rs 250 per day for each day of delay, subject to a maximum of Rs 25,000 (20(1)).

- If a PIO, without reasonable cause, refused to receive an application, malafidely denied information, knowingly gave incorrect, misleading or incomplete information, destroyed information, obstructed the provision of information, the PIO shall be liable to pay a penalty of Rs 250 per day till information is furnished, subject to a maximum of Rs 25,000 (20(1)).
- The Information Commission can also require the public authority that has illegitimately delayed/denied information to compensate the complainant for any loss or other detriment suffered (19(8)(b)).
- In case a PIO:
  i. without any reasonable cause and persistently, fails to receive an application for information or does not furnish information within the time specified,
  ii. or malafidely denies a request for information,
  iii. or knowingly gives incorrect, incomplete or misleading information,
  iv. or destroys information which is the subject of a request,
  v. or obstructs, in any manner, the furnishing of information,

  the information commission shall recommend disciplinary action against the concerned public information officer, under the service rules applicable to him/her (20(2)).

Some Definitions

"Information"

Information means any material held in any form with a government agency i.e., files, records i.e., tenders, contracts, agreements, MoUs, logbooks, notifications, GRs, orders, correspondence i.e., emails, letters, opinions, advice, samples, materials held in electronic formats, and as audio/visual materials (2(f)).

"Public authority"

Public Authority means any central or state government ministry, department, board, public sector undertaking (PSU), and any other organisation substantially financed directly or indirectly by the central/state government. Public authority also means any non-governmental organisation substantially financed directly or indirectly by the central/state government (2(h)).

Right to Information means:

- the right to seek information from any public authority,
- the right to take certified copies of records held by public authorities,
- the right to inspect records held by public authorities , take notes,
- the right to information also means the right to inspect any work being carried out by any public authority
- the right to take certified samples of material, and the right to take information in the form of tapes, floppies or held in any electronic format (2(j)).

II

Frequently Asked Questions

11. What is the Right to Information (RTI)?

The right to information is a fundamental right under Article 19(1) of the Constitution, which says that every citizen has a fundamental right to freedom of speech and expression. That the right to information is a fundamental right flowing from Article 19(1)(a) of the Constitution is now well settled. Over the years, the Supreme Court has consistently ruled in favour of the citizen's right to know. The nature of this right and the relevant restrictions thereto, has been discussed by the Supreme Court in a number of cases:

- In *Bennett Coleman v. Union of India*, (AIR 1973 SC 60), the right to information was held to be included within the right to freedom of speech and expression guaranteed by Art. 19(1) (a).
- In *State of UP v. Raj Narain*, ((1975) 4 SCC 428), the Court explicitly stated that it is not in the interest of the public to 'cover with a veil of secrecy the common routine business... the responsibility of officials to explain and to justify their acts is the

chief safeguard against oppression and corruption.'

- In *S.P. Gupta v. UOI*, (AIR 1982 SC 149), the right of the people to know about every public act, and the details of every public transaction undertaken by public functionaries was described.
- In Secretary Ministry of I&B, Govt. of India v. Cricket Assn. of Bengal, ((1995) 2 SCC 161), the right to impart and receive information from electronic media was included in the freedom of speech. The airwaves were held to be public property and hence distribution of these waves between government and private channels was to be done on an equitable basis.
- In People's Union for Civil Liberties v. UOI, (2004 (2) SCC 476), the right to information was further elevated to the status of a human right, necessary for making governance transparent and accountable. It was also emphasized that governance must be participatory.

12. *When did the RTI Act come into force?*

The national Right to Information Act came into force on the midnight of 12-13th October 2005. However, nine states already had state acts allowing access to information to varying degrees. These states were Jammu & Kashmir, Delhi, Rajasthan, Madhya Pradesh, Maharashtra, Karnataka, Tamil Nadu, Assam, & Goa.

13. *What happens to these state acts once the national act comes into force?*

A state has the freedom to retain or repeal its state act. So, for example, Delhi has not yet repealed its Right to Information act, while Maharashtra has. If a state does not repeal its act, then the state act can co-exist with the national act. People can apply for information under either their state act or under the national act. Where there is any conflict, the national act will prevail.

14. *What rights are available under RTI Act 2005?*

Right to Information Act 2005 empowers every citizen to-

- Seek and receive information from the government and other public authorities.
- Ask them certain questions.
- Take copies, including certified copies, of documents.
- Inspect documents.
- Inspect works.
- Take samples of materials. [Section 2 (j)]

15. *Who is covered under RTI?*

The Central RTI Act extends to the whole of India except the State of Jammu and Kashmir. It covers any authority or body or institution of self- government established or constituted

- by or under the Constitution;
- by any other law made by Parliament;
- by any other law made by State Legislature;
- by notification issued or order made by the appropriate Government, and includes any—

- body owned, controlled or substantially financed;
- non-Government organization substantially financed,

directly or indirectly by funds provided by the appropriate Government; [Section 1(2) & 2 (h)]

In short, all departments of the central, state and local governments, including urban municipalities and rural panchayati raj institutions, are covered. Also covered are all public sector units, all autonomous bodies owned, or controlled, or substantially financed, or set up by the government, all courts, from the Supreme Court to the local court, and the Parliament and legislative assemblies and councils.

16. *What is "substantially" financed?*

Though it is not defined, it should not be understood to mean "over 50 per cent". The correct approach might be to assume that all organizations that receive funding from the central or any state government or other public authority, directly or indirectly, are public authorities, governed by the RTI act. The onus can lie on any one of these organizations to establish that they are not public authorities because the support that they have received from the government is not substantial.

17. *What is "indirectly" financed?*

Where an NGO or other private entity (like a private hospital, school, college, temple, trust, society, etc.) gets, from the government, land at a concessional rate or free, or gets a tax or duty concession, or any other waiver or concession, then it can be understood to have been indirectly financed by the government. Similarly, if such an entity receives funds or concessions from an agency, which has been financed by the government, then that entity becomes indirectly financed by the government and the RTI act applies to it.

18. Are Private bodies covered under the RTI Act?

All private bodies that are substantially financed, directly or indirectly, by the government are already covered, as explained above. In addition, information can also be accessed, but via the government, from private bodies that are not financed by the government. Section 2(f) of the RTI act defines information as including "...information relating to any private body which can be accessed by a public authority under any other law for the time being in force;" This means that if a citizen wants information from, say, a private company, it can seek such information that the government or any public authority is entitled to access from that company under any other law. So, for example, the citizen can ask the department of company affairs to access and provide her information from the said company that that department can access under the Companies Act, or ask the income tax department to access under the Income Tax Law, or the labour department under any of the labour laws, or the environment department under any of the environmental laws. It is then the responsibility of the concerned department to access that information from the company and provide it to the citizen.

19. *Isn't the Official Secrets Act, 1923 an obstacle to the implementation of RTI Act?*

No. Section 22 of the RTI Act 2005 clearly says that the RTI Act would over ride all existing acts including the Officials Secrets Act. However, the continued existence of the Officials Secrets Act in its present form does have the potential to create confusion in the minds of the PIOs.

20. *How do I locate a copy of the full Act?*

The full Act in Hindi and English is available on the website of Department of Personnel and Training www.persmin.nic.in It is also available on www.righttoinformation.info

21. *Who can apply for information?*

Any citizen of India can apply for information under the RTI Act. There is no restriction on age and one or more persons can make an application [Section 3]. As per a recent Central Information Commission order, applications can also be on letterheads of organisations.

22. *How can I apply for information?*

Draft your application on a plain sheet of paper and submit it by post or in person to the Public Information Officer (PIO). [For details on how to file an application, see S.No. 4 above].

23. *Who will give me information?*

One or more officers in every public authority have been designated as Public Information Officers (PIO). These PIOs act like nodal officers. You have to file your applications with them. They are responsible for collecting information sought by you from various wings of that public authority and providing that information to you. In addition, several officials have been appointed as Assistant Public Information Officers (APIOs). Their job is only to accept applications and appeals from the public and forward it to the concerned PIO [For details see S. Nos. 3 & 4 above].

24. *Where do I submit an RTI application?*

You can do that with the PIO or with the APIO. In the case of all Central Government Departments, 629 post offices have been designated as APIOs. This means that you can go to any of these post offices and submit your fee and application at the RTI counter in these post offices. They will issue you a receipt and acknowledgement and it is the responsibility of that post office to deliver your application to the concerned PIO. The list of these post offices is given on the website http://www.indiapost.gov.in/rtimanual16a.html. State Governments are also required to designate APIOs at the sub-district levels. To get a list of such APIOs contact your state government or access their website [For details see S. No. 3 & 5 above].

25. *Is there any fee?*

Yes, there is an application fee. For Central Government Departments, it is Rs 10. However, different states and competent authorities have prescribed different fee. For getting photocopies, you have to pay Rs 2 per page for information provided by the Central Government Departments. It is different for different states. Similarly, there is a fee for inspection of documents. For the Central government, there is no fee for first hour of inspection, but after that you have to pay Rs. 5 for every subsequent hour or fraction thereof. (see annexure 1 for central government rules).

26. *How can I deposit my application fee?*

Every state has prescribed a different mode of payment for the application fee. Generally, you can deposit your application fee in person by paying cash [remember to get a receipt]. The central government has, in addition, allowed payment through demand draft, banker's cheque or postal order. In addition, various states have allowed payment through other means also, including treasury *challans*, money orders or court fee stamps [For details see S. No. 5 above].

27. *Can I submit my application only with the PIO?*

No, in case the PIO is not available you can submit your application with the Assistant PIO or any other officer designated to accept the RTI applications.

28. *Where can I locate the concerned PIO?*

A list of PIOs/APIOs and Appellate Authorities for all Central and State departments/Ministries is available online at www.rti.gov.in

How to Find Your PIO

To find your APIO, PIO, or Appellate Authority for a Central Government Agency, simply go to http://rti.gov.in/ You can access both Union and State Government PIO/APIO details from this website.

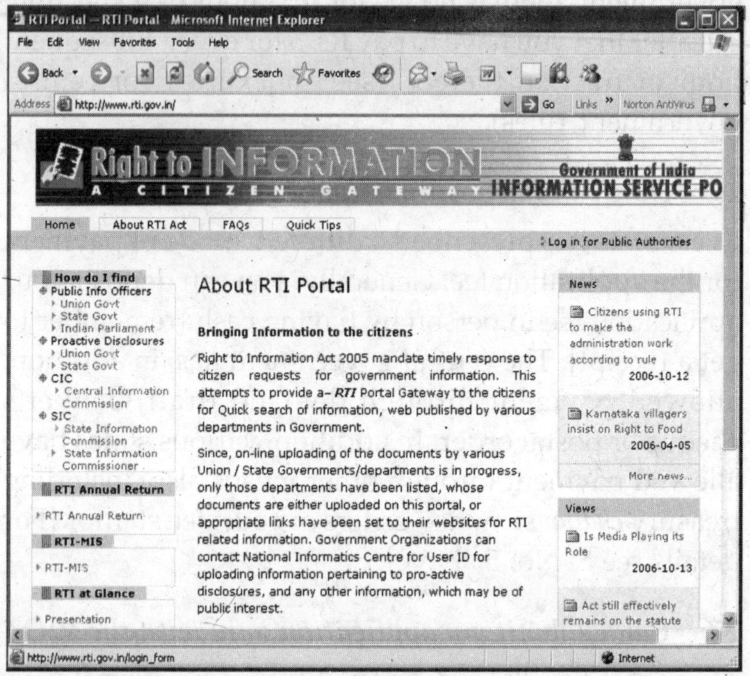

29. *What if I cannot locate my PIO or APIO?*

In case you have problems locating your PIO/APIO you can address your RTI application to the PIO, c/o Head of Department and send it to the concerned public authority with the requisite application fee. The Head of Department will have to forward your application to the concerned PIO.

30. *Do I have to personally go to deposit my application?*

Depending on the rules applicable for mode of payment, you can deposit your application for information with the concerned public authority either by hand or via post by attaching a DD, Money Order,

Postal Order or affixing Court fee Stamp.

For all Central government departments the Department of Posts has designated 629 postal offices at the national level. The designated officers in these post offices work as Assistant PIOs and collect the application to forward to the concerned PIO. A list is available on:

http://www.indiapost.gov.in/rticontents.html

31. *Is there a time limit within which the information I asked for is to be provided?*

Yes. If you file your application with the PIO, you must ordinarily receive information within 30 days. In case you have filed your application with an Assistant PIO then information has to be made available within 35 days.In case the matter to which the information pertains affects the life and liberty of an individual, information has to be made available in 48 hours [For details see S. No. 6 above].

32. *Can the PIO refuse to accept my RTI application?*

There are only a few situations under which the PIO can legitimately refuse to accept your application. These include:

1) If the application is addressed to some other PIO/ Public Authority.
2) If you are unable/unwilling to pay the prescribed fee in the prescribed manner.
3) If you are seeking exemption of fee as a member of a BPL family but cannot provide the prescribed documentation/ proof.

33. ***There have been many good laws in this country but none of those laws worked. Why do you think this law would work?***

For the first time the people who are affected directly by corruption and other forms of bad governance are being themselves empowered to do something about it. This is clearly a great improvement on earlier laws where action was expected from people who were not directly affected but only elected/appointed to perform this task. In any case, the rapidly growing use and popularity of the RTI Act is in itself evidence of its popularity and effectiveness.

BB gets his gas cylinder by using RTI

BB of Darrang district, Assam came to know that Assam Government is distributing gas cylinder free of cost to the poor people. The boy who informed him said that Rs. 500/ would have to be paid to get the gas cylinder. BB was not willing to pay this amount. After a few days some people in his village got new gas cylinders free of cost. Though BB was the poorest among them, he did not get a cylinder. In the mean time, he came to know about Right to Information Act 2005. He immediately filed an RTI application asking for the list of beneficiaries under the scheme. To his utter surprise he discovered that his name was at the top of the list of beneficiaries. There were 17 beneficiaries but only 10 had been allotted the gas cylinders. Empowered with this information, BB complained to the DC of Darrang district. The result was immediate. All the 17 beneficiaries immediately got the gas cylinder and the concerned officer has been suspended. Now BB has become a household name in the locality.

34. *What can I do if I do not receive information?*

If you do not receive information or are dissatisfied with the information received, you can file an appeal with the first appellate authority under section 19 (1) of the Right to Information Act [For details see S. No. 7 above].

35. *Who is a First Appellate authority?*

Every public authority must designate a First Appellate Authority. This officer is senior in rank to the PIO [For details see S. No. 7 above].

36. *Is the Assistant Public Information Officer obliged to accept the first/second appeal?*

Under Section 5(2) of the RTI Act, the Central/State APIO is obliged to receive and forward first as well as second appeal applications to the concerned authorities. However, an additional time of five days will be added to the time limit prescribed for the disposal of the first appeal [For details see S. No. 3 above].

37. *Is there a form for the first appeal?*

This differs from state to state and public authority to public authority.

38. *Do I have to pay a fee for the first appeal?*

This differs from state to state and public authority to public authority.

39. *In how many days can I file my first appeal?*

You can file your first appeal within 30 days of expiry of the period within which you should have received the information or if the information has been refused, within 30 days of the refusal.

40. *How can the use of the RTI Act help me?*

The RTI Act can be helpful in many ways, both to you individually and through you to the larger society. For example:

a) You can use the RTI Act to access information that you were finding difficult/ impossible to find. For example: you can use this Act to find out what is the status of your application for a job, membership, license etc.

b) You can also find out the reasons why certain things were denied to you or why delays took place.

c) For ongoing matters, you can find out the status of the matter, reasons for delay, if any, the officials responsible, and use this information to ensure that the work is done at the earliest.

d) You can also access information, collect samples, or conduct inspections in order to ensure that public works have been/are being properly done and through this bring accountability to public servants and public services.

e) You can use the RTI to expose past or on going corruption or poor governance, thereby deterring future corruption.

41. ***Is the amount recovered from the PIO as fine / penalty given to the aggrieved applicant?***

No. Fines and penalties are deposited into the public account. However, under sec 19 (8)(b) the applicant can be compensated for any loss or other detriment suffered.

III

Common Questions Posed by RTI Applicants

42. ***What can you do if the name and address of the PIO is not available?***

Send the RTI application to the head of the public authority with the request to forward the same to the PIO, as his/her details are not publicly available. A copy should also be sent to the Information Commission for necessary action under section 19(a)(ii) of the RTI Act.

Under Section 5(2) there should be an APIO for every single public authority. In case Central/State government has not designated an APIO that reasonably covers your area, you can complain to the Central/State Information Commission and request them to take action under section 19(8)(a).

43. ***What can you do if the application / application fee is refused by a public authority?***

Send the application to the PIO by registered acknowledgement due post, clearly marking on the outside of the envelope that it is an application under the RTI Act 2005. If this is also refused, then a complaint under Section 18(1) should be made to the Information Commission, along with copies of relevant documents establishing that your application, sent by registered post, was refused. You can demand that the concerned PIO is penalized under section 20(1). Though all unreasonable refusals are punishable under the RTI act, without documentary proof it is often difficult to prove that your application was refused.

44. *Can the PIO/public authority insist that you come back another day/time to submit your application/ fee?*

Under the law they are obliged to receive your application during the time specified for the purpose by the public authority or, if no time is specified, during office hours, otherwise it would tantamount to a refusal (see S.No. 32 above). Therefore, if you attempted to file your application during the time specified or during office hours and have been asked to come back another time/day, you could proceed as suggested in S.No. 43 above.

45. *Can they send back your application saying that it concerns another department?*

If the information you have asked for wholly or partly concerns another PIO/public authority, it is the responsibility of the PIO/public authority to transfer you application (in full or part) to the concerned department, within five days, as specified in section 6(3) of the RTI act.

46. *What can you do if they insist that you submit your RTI request in a specific format?*

The law does not allow public authorities to insist on a specific format. [This has also been upheld by the Central Information Commission vide their order on the review application No CIC/C/I/2006 dated 30.01.06, Madhu Bhaduri vs DDA]. However, public authorities are free to suggest a format, which you can use if you so desire.

47. *If you are illiterate or otherwise unable to write, can you still file an RTI application?*

Section 6(1) clearly obligates the PIO to render all reasonable assistance to reduce the request for information in writing. Section 7(4) of the law also makes it obligatory to provide the required assistance to persons who are sensorily disabled. In general, the law obligates the PIO to render all reasonable assistance to persons seeking information (Section 5(3)).

48. *Can the PIO or any other person demand to know why we want the information that we are asking for and / or to what use are we going to put it?*

Section 6(2) clearly states that no applicant will be required to give any reason for requesting the information.

49. *Can the PIO or any other person insists that we provide, along with our application, details about ourselves, like our job, income, education qualification, caste, marital status, proof of citizenship, etc.?*

Section 6(2) specifically prohibits seeking any personal

details of the applicant except those that may be necessary for contacting the applicant. You could be asked to certify that you are an Indian citizen but cannot be asked to submit proof of your citizenship. However, if you are seeking exemption of fee as a member of a BPL family under section 7(5), then you could be required to provide the prescribed document/proof of your being below the poverty line.

50. *What should you do if the public authority charges you exorbitantly for photocopying or asks you to pay for the letters they have written you?*

You should check the fee rules, as photocopying rates are specified in the fee rules and must be charged as per the rules. If the number of pages being charged for seem unreasonable, you can seek to inspect the relevant papers and select those which you want copies of. If the public authority insists that this will be treated as a fresh request for information, then you can either pay the required additional fee for the fresh request or file a complaint with the Information Commission under section 18(1) (d).

51. *Can the public authority ask for other processing fees?*

[For example under Section 7(3)(a) of the RTI Act 2005]. The fees chargeable have to be specified in the fee rules. No fee can be charged which has not been specified in the fee rules or is in variance with what the rules specify.

52. ***What should you do if the PIO / public authority summons you for a meeting?***

The law does not authorise public authorities to summon applicants for meetings or even insist that the applicant personally collects the information asked for. You only need to collect the information in person if you have indicated your preference to do so. However, you might consider responding to requests for meetings, even though not required to by law, in order to facilitate the provision of information.

53. ***What should you do if you are approached or threatened by people who want you to withdraw your application or not pursue it?***

There is a danger that you would be subjected to threats if the information you have sought relates to powerful or unruly vested interests. This should always be kept in mind and where the danger is real and the information sought is not covered under the privacy clause, the information can always be sought in the name of another person who might not be easily threatened or resides in some far of place.

Where the type of information being sought affects more than one person, it is sometimes advisable to seek it jointly with other people so that numbers can give you strength and protection.

If, despite all precautions, you are still threatened you should not only take all required precautions but also immediately report the matter to the appropriate police station, with copies to the heads of the relevant public authorities and to the concerned Information Commission.

54. *What should you do if you are approached with the promise that your grievance would be resolved if you withdraw your RTI application, or if the grievance / issue is actually resolved before you receive the asked for information?*

Barring some exceptions, it would be advisable to pursue your RTI application, for this would ensure that not only your specific grievance but also the systemic reasons behind the grievance are addressed.

55. *What can you do if information is not received within the prescribed time period?*

Concurrently, you can file a first appeal under section 19 (1), with the appellate authority within the public authority, and a complaint under section 18(1) (c) with the Information Commission

As per section 7(6), information provided after the prescribed time period will be made available free of charge – and the application fee and all other charges will be waived or reimbursed.

56. *What should you do if there is no response to an urgent application under section 7(1) (the "life or liberty" clause)?*

File an urgent appeal with the Information Commission requesting for an immediate hearing. This is in keeping with a recent decision of the Central Information Commission on appeal no. CIC/WB/C/2006/00066 dated 19.04.06, Shekhar Singh, Aruna Roy and others vs PMO

57. *What should you do if the public authority denies information wholly / partly?*

Examine the reasons for denial and if you find the reasons unacceptable then file a first appeal with the first appellate authority under section 19(1) [For details see S.No. 7 above].

58. *How do I find out whom to appeal to?*

The PIO is obligated in his response to you [vide section 7(3)(b) & section 7(8)(ii & iii)] to inform you of the particulars of the first appellate authority, time limit for appeal, the appeal process and whether any forms are required for the appeal.

59. *What can you do if the public authority claims that your request for information has been fulfilled in accordance with the RTI act, however in your opinion the information you asked for was:*
- *Delayed without any reasonable cause,*
- *Malafidely denied*
- *Knowingly incorrect,*
- *Knowingly Incomplete, or*
- *Knowingly Misleading [S 20(1)]?*

You can go in first appeal under section 19 (1) and can concurrently file a complaint with the Information Commission under section 18 (1) [For details see S.No. 7 above].

60. *What can you do if a public authority denies your request and claims that it does not have the required information?*

If the information is genuinely not with them or with

any other public authority, and they are not required to collect the information, then the denial is justified. No further appeal is advised.

If the information is not with them but with some other public authority then they are obliged under section 6(3) of the RTI act to forward your application to the concerned public authority, within 5 days of receiving it.

If the information is not with them, despite the fact that they are supposed to collect the information as per law/policy/orders/regulations etc., and have not done so, then they are obliged to collect the information and provide it to you. This should be done, if necessary, by the PIO writing to those persons/public authorities that have this information. The PIO should inform these persons/ public authorities that the information is required under the RTI Act, the time frame within which it is to be provided, and their liability under section 5(5).

61. *Can you get certified copies of documents?*

Under Section 2(j)(ii) you are entitled to certified copies of documents/records, but it is advisable to specify in your original application that you require certified copies.

62. *What happens if the response is not signed by the PIO/APIO?*

As long as the reply is an official reply signed by an official of the public authority, it should be considered valid.

63. *Is the first Appellate Authority required to hear you before disposing your appeal?*

As per the RTI Act, the first appellate authority is not obliged to call you for the first appeal, unless the appeal rules for the state/authority require so. However, natural justice demands that the concerned parties be given an opportunity to be heard.

64. *What should you do if you disagree with the first Appellate Authority's decision in part or whole?*

File a second appeal with the Central or State Information Commission, as relevant, under section 19(3) in the formats prescribed, if any, by the relevant Information Commissions. Also see appeal rules for Centre and State [For details see S. No. 8 above, and Annexure 3 for Central Information Commission second appeal format].

65. *What should you do if the first Appellate Authority does not respond within 45 days?*

Confirm if your appeal has been disposed off or not and ask for a copy of the order, as is your right under the law. If it has not, file an appeal with the Central or State Information Commissions [see annexure 2 for rules of the centre –for further details see S.No. 8 above, and annexure 3 for CIC second appeal format].

66. *What can you do if the Central / State Information Commission does not respond to your second appeal application?*

Unfortunately, there is no time limit under the Act for the disposal of second appeals. Therefore, you need to contact the Information Commission and find out the status of your appeal. If it has been inordinately delayed, you should write to the information commission requesting them to urgently hear it. You also have the option of approaching the High/Supreme Court for relief.

67. ***Is the Information Commission required to give you an opportunity of being heard, while disposing your appeal?***

The procedure for disposing appeals is laid out in the appeal rules. However, principles of natural justice demand that all concerned persons be given an opportunity to be heard before the matter is disposed off. (Please see the appeal rules at annexure 3; also see WP(C) 1522/2007 Yago Rangatia vs the CIC, Delhi High Court).

68. ***What happens if I am unable to attend the hearing / do not feel confident that I could argue my own case adequately before the information commission?***

The central and many state rules permit your nominating somebody else to appear on your behalf or to accompany you or assist you in your hearing. However, you are not required to be present or represented while your appeal is being heard, and your appeal should be dealt with on merit even otherwise.

69. ***What course of action is open to you if you are dissatisfied with the outcome of your second appeal?***

Consider one or both of the following options:

- Apply for a review to the Chief Information Commissioner giving detailed reasons why you are dissatisfied with the order.
- Go to the High Court/ Supreme Court in appeal in Writ petition.

Note: You cannot appeal to the Central Information Commission against an order of any of the state information commissions.

70. ***Can you be compensated for illegitimate delays and / or denial of information that caused you harassment and / or loss?***

Under section 19(8)(b) the Information Commissions can require the public authority concerned to compensate you for any loss or other detriment suffered (See, for example, appeal No. CIC/OK/A/2006/00163; Decision No. 519/IC(A)/2007; Decision No. 458/IC(A)/2006 on www.cic.gov.in).

71. ***Can personal information about an individual be given out without consulting him / her?***

No. Under section 11 the PIO is obliged to inform the third party, if there is an intention to release private information about a third party which has been treated as confidential by the third party. The third party also has a right to be heard in the matter and, further, if required, to appeal in the matter.

72. ***What is the difference between an appeal and a complaint? Can both be filed together?***

An appeal is made against the order of a Public Information Officer, or against the lack of response by the PIO in the prescribed time frame (deemed refusal under Section 7(2)), to the first appellate authority and similarly against the orders of the first appellate authority to the Information Commission. The appeal basically seeks to wholly or partially overturn the order appealed against or obtain an order providing for access to information.

A Complaint, on the other hand, is made only to the information commission against only the PIO for violating the law in one or more of the ways listed in Section 20(1), specifically for refusing to accept an RTI application (this also against APIOs), for delaying information without reasonable grounds, for malafidely denying the request for information, for knowingly giving incorrect, incomplete or misleading information, for destroying information which was the subject of the request, or for obstructing in any manner in furnishing the information.

Under the law, you can file appeals and complaints concurrently. The former can be filed with the first appellate at the same time that the latter is filed with the Information Commission. For example, if the PIO has not responded to you within 30 days, you can file an appeal against this deemed refusal to the first appellate authority, while filing a complaint for delay with the Information Commission. In case the final decision is that the information asked for cannot be given to you, the Information Commission can still impose penalties on the PIO for not communicating to you within the prescribed time frame the denial of the information asked for.

A penalty can be imposed either as a result of a specific complaint received and inquired into under Section 18(1) & (2) of the RTI Act. It can also be imposed, under section 20(1), even without a specific complaint, if the Information Commission is of the opinion, while disposing off an appeal, that a penalty is called for.

73. ***Can information be made public that is marked secret under the Official Secrets Act?***

Under Section 22, wherever there is a conflict between provisions of the Official Secrets Act 1923, or indeed of any other law, and the Right to Information act 2005, the RTI Act shall prevail. Therefore, only that information can be withheld, which is exempt under the RTI Act. It is irrelevant what classification it has been given, or indeed, if it is marked secret under the Official Secrets Act.

74. ***Are any organisations exempt under the RTI Act?***

Under Section 24, read with the Second Schedule, various intelligence and security organisations are exempt from furnishing information under the RTI Act. However, section 24(1) & (4) specifies that this exemption does not cover information pertaining to allegations of corruption and/or human rights violation in any of these organisations.

75. ***What happens if the information required to be made public* suo motu *under section 4 has not been made public?***

A complaint should be made to the Information Commissions to issue appropriate recommendations as per section 25(5). An application can also be filed with the PIO asking for the suo moto publication of the required information, in accordance with the law. In case the application and first appeal do not get the required results, an appeal can be filed with the information commission, and the information commission can require the public authority to publish such information (19(8)(a)) and impose penalties under section 19 ((8)(c), if they still do not comply.

IV

FAQs Posed by Public Authorities and PIOs/APIOs

76. *What are our obligations under section 4 of the RTI Act?*

Section 4 mainly deals with the obligations of the public authority to maintain, computerize and *suo moto* publish certain types of information. The details are given in the RTI Act. Broadly they fall into the following heads:

- Properly maintaining, indexing and cataloguing all records (section 4(1)(a)).
- Computerising and networking available information (section 4(1)(a)).
- Publishing *suo moto* organisational details, supervision and decision making processes, norms, rules, regulations, guidelines, list of the categories of documents available, details about public participation, list/ composition/details of committees and bodies, list and other details of officers/staff, budgets, details of schemes, subsidies, programmes, grants, permits, and concessions, etc. (section 4(1)(b)).

- Publishing *suo moto* details of the PIOs/APIOs, appellate authorities etc. under the RTI act (section 4(1)(b)).
- Publishing *suo moto* other details relating to access to information (section 4(1)(b)).
- Publishing *suo moto* all relevant facts while formulating important policies or announcing the decisions, which affect public (section 4(1)(c)).
- Providing reasons for its administrative or quasi-judicial decisions to affected persons (section 4(1)(d)).

77. ***What should you do if the application pertains wholly / partly to some other public authority / PIO?***

Under section 6(3) you are required to transfer the application to the concerned PIO/public authority, within 5 days, under intimation to the applicant. The application fee can be retained but it should be indicated in the letter transferring the application, that it has been received.

78. ***What is the PIO expected to do if the applicant approaches the PIO with an oral request but is illiterate or otherwise unable to reduce the request into writing?***

Section 6(1) clearly obligates the PIO to render all reasonable assistance to reduce the request for information in writing. The law also obligates the PIO to render all reasonable assistance to persons seeking information (Section 5(3))

79. ***Are you obliged to/ permitted to ask the applicant why he / she wants the information and / or what use will they put it to?***

Section 6(2) clearly states that no applicant will be required to give any reason for requesting the information.

80. ***Are you obliged to / permitted to ask the applicant for details about their job, income, education qualification, caste, marital status, proof of citizenship?***

Sections 6(2) specifically prohibits seeking any personal details of the applicant except those that may be necessary for contacting the applicant.

81. ***What are your obligations when you respond to an application?***

The PIO is obliged in her response [vide Section 7(3)(b)& Section 7(8)] to inform the applicant of the further fee to be paid, if any, and the applicants right with respect to review of the decision as to the amount of fees charged or the form of access provided, including the particulars of the appellate authority, time limit, process and any other forms, the fees for the appeal and, where there is a rejection, the reasons for rejecting.

82. ***What happens if the application does not clearly specify the information being asked for?***

While receiving the application you should get a clarification from the applicant what exactly is required, and if necessary request him to rewrite the application. Otherwise, an effort should be made to contact the applicant over the telephone, if possible, to seek clarifications. In case that is not possible, then the applicant should be contacted by post and requested to send a clarification as soon as possible (5(3)).

83. *What should you do if the application contains a large number of queries, which are unrelated to each other?*

The Act provides for a single application for information per payment of a specified fee. Where the applicant asks multiple questions relating to the same matter/issue, these should be treated as a single application. However, where information is sought for a multiple set of unrelated issues the first set of related questions should be processed and, for the remaining, the applicant should be advised to file separate applications for each independent issue/subject.

84. *What happens if the applicant requires information in a form that would be very time consuming / costly to provide?*

Under the RTI Act, you have the option of providing information in the form that it is available rather than in the form asked for, if the latter disproportionately diverts the resources of your office. However, this does not allow the PIO to refuse information altogether on this ground [section 7 (9)].

For example, if somebody asks for information in a collated form, which is only available in a disaggregated form, and if the collation would disproportionately divert the resources of the department, then the PIO is within the law in offering to provide the information in the disaggregated form that it is available.

> If one asks under the RTI the question: how many of the patients treated for tuberculosis in Delhi government hospitals, during 2005-06, were smokers? There are three alternatives:
>
> 1. Such information is not collected from the patients, and therefore the government can inform the applicant that this information is not available.
> 2. Or, though it is collected from each patient, it is neither compiled for the whole of Delhi, nor is such a compilation obligatory. In this case, the public authority can compile it, if this is not too laborious and time consuming, or provide to the applicant the disaggregated data, which the applicant will have to compile herself.
> 3. If it is collected and compiled, then it can be provided in the form asked for.

85. What is the PIOs liability in terms of penalties, if the information asked for is with some other officer who, despite best efforts, does not respond or does not respond in time?

Section 5(5) clearly states that any officer whose assistance has been sought shall render all assistance to the PIO seeking his or her assistance and for the purposes of any contravention of the provisions of this Act, such other officer shall be treated as a Public Information Officer. Therefore, the liability for delay or other violation shifts to the officer who has delayed or otherwise contravened provisions of the act. **The PIO is not liable for the delay or violation by others.**

86. ***Can one summarily reject applications that appear to be frivolous, vexatious, or appear to be aimed at harassing or blackmailing officials?***

The Act is very clear and specific about the types of information that can be exempted. It does not permit applications being rejected because they appear to be frivolous and/or vexatious. Besides, what might appear frivolous or vexatious to the PIO might be of critical importance to the applicant.

As the Right to Information only allows the dissemination of the truth, it is not possible to use the information so acquired to harass or blackmail officials. Officials can only be adversely affected by information so procured if they have indulged in some unlawful acts. Besides, blackmail is only possible where the blackmailer(s) has privileged access to some information, which is not available to others. However, information accessed under the RTI Act is freely available to all citizens of India and, therefore, cannot be systematically used for blackmail.

87. ***On what basis does one decide whether the information asked for can be provided or not?***

All the exclusions allowed under the law are listed under section 8(1), section 9, section 24(1)&(4). Any information that is not specifically excluded under these sections cannot be denied to an applicant. However, it must be kept in mind that all these exemptions are subject to the general proviso at the end of section 8(1) regarding the parliamentary/state legislature test, and regarding public interest override and freer access to information that is older than 20 years, as further specified in section 8(2)&(3), .

It must also be remembered that if there is an appeal, then the onus to prove whether denial of request was justified shall be on the PIO (section 19(5)). Similarly, if a complaint is made for imposition of penalties under section 20, then again the onus to prove that the PIO acted reasonably and diligently shall be the PIOs (section 20(1))

88. *What should the PIO do if a record asked for contains portions, which are exempt under the Act?*

Section 10 specifically provides for severing those portions that contain exempt information/record and making the remainder of the information available.

89. *Can personal information be given out to an applicant without consulting the person that it relates to?*

Before providing any information under this Act the PIO must satisfy herself that this information is not third party information, as defined under Section 11, which has been treated as confidential by the third party. In case it is, the PIO will have to ensure that the procedures laid down under section 11 for giving an opportunity for being heard have been followed and that the information can still be disclosed (7(7)).

90. *In deciding whether a record should be provided to an applicant or not, is it permissible to consult colleagues/seniors?*

Whereas, there is no bar to such consultation, this would not absolve the PIO of the responsibility of the final decision, unless the decision is based on a response, in writing, from a superior officer in the form of a direction or from the officer who holds the required information and has declined to provide it.

However, it is not permissible for a PIO to formally take the concurrence of the first Appellate Authority before refusing the request for information, thereby circumventing or making redundant the process of first appeal, as prescribed under the law.

91. ***Is the PIO always liable for a fine if the information is not provided within the prescribed time frame or are there exceptions?***

Penalty for refusing to receive an application or for furnishing information later than the time specified under section 7(1) can be avoided if the PIO can establish that the refusal/delay had a reasonable cause. Though the term "reasonable cause" is not defined in the law it is commonly understood to include factors that are beyond the control of the PIO, despite making all the possible and required effort. However, this is not commonly understood to include ignorance and/ or misunderstanding of the law, pre-occupation with other work, and giving low importance to RTI matters.

Penalties relating to the provision of incorrect, incomplete, or misleading information, or destruction of sought-after information, can only be avoided if it can be shown that this was done unknowingly. However, as already stated earlier, the burden of proof would be on the PIO.

Wrong denial of information would invariably attract a penalty unless it can be established by the PIO that there was no malafide intent. This would involve establishing, at the very least, that the denial was due to a genuine interpretation of the law or of facts, which might be mistaken but could reasonably be held.

92. *What is the liability of the public authority if the records asked for have been destroyed?*

There is no legal liability on the public authority as long as these records have been destroyed in accordance with the established policy of the department for the destruction of records, subject to directions, if any by the Information commission vide section 19(8)(a)(iv).

93. *Must old records also be made available to applicants under this act or is there a time limit beyond which records are exempt from disclosure?*

RTI power: Ex-FCI executive gets files after 20 years

Twenty years after the CBI chargesheeted him in a corruption case K, a 73-year-old former staffer of the Food Corporation of India (FCI), has finally succeeded in gaining access to two official reports in the custody of his ex-paymaster which may help him "conclude" the long-pending matter, all due to the Right to Information Act.

"He (K) is seeking inspection of the files which relate to a period 20 years before the date of his application under the Act, FCI cannot deny the information," the Information Commissioner said in the order passed.

K believes that the files recording the probe held against him in 1984 may aid his vindication in the case.

The matter has been pending in a Patna court for the past two decades and Kohli has already attended over 240 hearings held there in this regard.

There is no time limit and, in fact, section 8(3) specifies that information regarding events that have occurred 20 years or more before the date they are requested must be freely given except where such information is exempt under section 8(1)(a), (c) and (i), because its disclosure might compromise the sovereignty and integrity of India, the security, strategic, scientific or economic interests of the State, relation with foreign State or lead to incitement of an offence; or violate Parliamentary or legislative privilege, or cabinet deliberations that are still ongoing.

94. ***What action is required if a record asked for is misplaced / not traceable?***

a) A proper search has to be instituted.

b) If the record is still untraceable, the responsibility has to be fixed.

c) As far as possible, the record has to reconstructed and provided and.

d) Recent orders of the Central Information Commission have highlighted the fact that where records are deemed to be misplaced/not traceable then, as a minimum a First Information Report (F.I.R) needs to be filed. *[Appeal No. CIC/WB/C/2006/00102 dated 9/6/'06, Ms. Misha Singh vs Ministry of Environment & Forests]*

95. *What is the difference between an appeal and complaint? Can both be filed together?*

An appeal is made against the order of a Public Information Officer, or against the lack of response by the PIO in the prescribed time frame (deemed refusal under Section 7(2)), to the first appellate authority and similarly against the orders of the first appellate authority to the Information Commission. The appeal basically seeks to wholly or partially overturn the order appealed against or obtain an order providing for access to information.

A Complaint, on the other hand, is made only to the information commission against only the PIO for violating the law in one or more of the ways listed in Section 20(1), specifically for refusing to accept an RTI application (this also against APIOs), for delaying information without reasonable grounds, for malafidely denying the request for information, for knowingly giving incorrect, incomplete or misleading information, for destroying information which was the subject of the request, or for obstructing in any manner in furnishing the information.

Under the law, you can file appeals and complaints concurrently. The former can be filed with the first appellate at the same time that the latter is filed with the Information Commission. For example, if the PIO has not responded within 30 days, you can file an appeal against this deemed refusal to the first appellate authority, while filing a complaint for delay with the Information Commission. In case the final decision is that the information asked for cannot be given to you, the Information Commission can still impose penalties on the PIO for not communicating to you within the prescribed time frame the denial of the information asked for.

A penalty can be imposed either as a result of a specific complaint received and inquired into under Section 18(1) & (2) of the RTI Act. It can also be imposed, under section 20(1), even without a specific complaint, if the Information Commission is of the opinion, while disposing an appeal, that a penalty is called for.

96. What happens if a PIO discloses information that his superiors subsequently consider to be exempt?

Where the PIO has acted in good faith, no suit, prosecution or other legal proceedings can lie against her (Section 20(1)).

97. Can information be made public that is marked secret under the Official Secrets Act?

Under Section 22, wherever there is a conflict between provisions of the Official Secrets Act 1923, or indeed of any other law etc., and the Right to Information Act 2005, the RTI Act shall prevail. Only that information can be withheld, which is exempt under the RTI Act. Therefore, whether it is marked secret or not under the Official Secrets Act is irrelevant.

98. ***Are any organisations exempt under the RTI Act?***

Under Section 24 read with the Second Schedule, various intelligence and security organisations are exempt from furnishing information under the RTI Act. However, under Section 24(1)&(4) this exemption does not cover information pertaining to allegations of corruption and/or human rights violation in any of these organisations.

Annexure 1

SAMPLE RTI APPLICATION TO FOLLOW UP ON AN APPLICATION OR COMPLAINT

To
The Public Information Officer,
____

Sub: Application under Right to Information Act 2005

I had made an application/complaint for the following reason (copy of application/complaint is attached) but no action/satisfactory action has been taken on my application so far.

Please provide the following information with respect to the same:

1. Please indicate the daily progress made on my application/complaint so far. i.e. when did my application/complaint reach which officer, for how long did it stay with that officer and what action did he/she take on it during that period?
2. Please give the names and designations of the officials, if any, who delayed taking action on my application/complaint.
3. What action would be taken against these officials for delay? By when would that action be taken?

4. By when would my application/complaint be dealt with?

I am separately depositing Rs   as application fee.

Yours sincerely,

IF THEY REPLY SAYING THAT YOUR APPLICATION/COMPLAINT HAS NOT BEEN DELAYED AND IS BEING DEALT WITH IN THE REQUIRED MANNNER THEN YOU CAN ASK FOR TWO TYPES OF THINGS:

1. The norms, if any, prescribed for the department to deal with these types of applications/complaints.
2. List of any applications/complaints/ that were received after your application/complaint but dealt with earlier, and the reasons thereof.

IF THIS INFORMATION ESTABLISHES THAT YOUR APPLICATION/COMPLAINT HAS BEEN DELAYED BEYOND THE PRESCRIBED TIMEFRAME OR THAT OTHER APPLICATIONS/COMPLAINTS HAVE BEEN DEALT WITH FASTER THAN YOURS, YOU CAN THEN FILE A COMPLAINT WITH THE HEAD OF THE DEPARTMENT. IF ACTION ON THIS COMPLAINT IS ALSO DELAYED THEN FILE AN RTI AS SUGGESTED ABOVE.

SAMPLE RTI APPLICATION TO INSPECT FILES

To
The Public Information Officer,
____

Sub: Application under Right to Information Act 2005

I had applied for the transfer of ownership of land, as per details given below, to my name vide my letter dated ————— (copy enclosed).

As per section 2(j)(i) of the Right to Information Act 2005. I wish to inspect all the files related to this issue, including file notings etc. Kindly let me know at the earliest the location of the files and the date, time and venue where I can come and inspect the files.

I am depositing Rs.—— as application fee

Yours sincerely,

SAMPLE RTI APPLICATION SEEKING INFORMATION ABOUT A SPECIFIC ISSUE

To
The Public Information Officer
____

Subject: Application under the Right to Information Act 2005

Please provide the following information:

1. Please provide a list of all the properties, which are being used for commercial purposes, in X Colony,
2. How many of these colonies are in violation of building bylaws?
3. Please intimate the nature of violation in each case.
4. When did each of this violation first come to the knowledge of Department?
5. What are the departmental guidelines under which it can initiate action against such violation? Please provide a certified copy of these guidelines.
6. Did the department initiate any inquiry or action against these violations?
7. Please indicate in detail the process followed by the MCD for taking action against such violation. If an inquiry was conducted please provide a certified copy of the inquiry report.
8. If no steps have been taken in any case, please

provide reasons for inaction on behalf of the Department.

9. Please provide the names, designations and contact details of the officials who have the duty to take action against these violations.

I am depositing Rs. 10 as application fee

Yours sincerely,

SAMPLE RTI APPLICATION SEEKING LIST OF NAMES/BENEFICIARIES ETC.

To
The Public Information Officer,
____

Sub: Application under Right to Information Act 2005

Please provide me the following information (for example one of the following):

1. Name and address of all those who have been allotted petrol pumps in the last five years from the discretionary quota, along with the reasons why such an allotment was made in each case.

OR

2. List of people who have been issued BPL Antodaya cards along with the basis on which each one of them has been so selected.

OR

3. Names and addresses of those who have been given any benefits under the Indira Awas Yojana and the basis on which they have been selected.

OR

4. Names and addresses of those who have been issues job cards in my village under the NREGA.

I am depositing Rs. as application fee.

Yours sincerely,

SAMPLE RTI APPLICATION SEEKING SAMPLES OF MATERIALS

To
The Public Information Officer
____

Subject: Application under the Right to Information Act 2005

As per section 2(j)(iii) of the Right to Information Act, 2005 would like to get a sample of (any one of the following)

1. The bitumen used to carper the road between village X and Y, block ——, tehsil ——
2. Mid day meals being served in school—, village ——.
3. Milk being distributed by Mother Dairy in booth no. ——

The sample should be collected in my presence and should be sealed and certified. Please intimate the date, time and venue where I should come to witness the collection of the samples.

I am depositing Rs. 10 as application fee.

Yours sincerely

Annexure

(TO BE PUBLISHED IN PART II, SECTION 3, SB SECTION (I) OF THE GAZETTE OF INDIA

Government of India

Ministry of Personnel, Public Grievances and Pensions

(Department of Personnel and Training)

New Delhi dated the 16th September, 2005

NOTIFICATION

G.S.R......., in exercise of the powers conferred by clauses(b) and (c) of Sub section (2) of Section 27 of the Right to Information Act, 2005 (22 of 2005), the Central Government makes the following rules, namely :-

1. Short title and commencement – (1) these rules may be called the Right to Information (Regulation of Fees and Cost)Rules, 2005.

(2) They shall come into force on the date of their publication in the official gazette.

2. Definitions- In the rules, unless the context otherwise requires,-
   - (a) "Act" means the Right to Information Act, 2005.
   - (b) "Section" means section of the Act.
   - (c) all other words and expressions used herein but not defined and defined the act shall have the meanings assigned to them in the Act.

3. A request for obtaining information under subsection (1) of Section 6 shall be accompanied by an application fee of Rs. 10/- by way of cash against proper receipt or by demand draft or bankers cheque payable to the Accounts officer of the Public authority.

4. For providing the information under Subsection(1) of section 7, the fee shall be charged by way of cash against proper receipt or by demand draft or bankers cheque payable to the Accounts Officer of the public authority at the following rates:-

   (a) Rs. 2/- for each page (in A-4 or A-3 size paper), created or copied;

   (b) actual charge or cost price of a copy in larger size paper;

   (c) actual cost or price for samples or models; and

   (d) for inspection of records, no fee for the first hour; and the fee of Rs. 5/- for each fifteen minutes (or fraction thereof) thereafter.

5. For providing the information under Sub section (5) of Secton 7, the fee shall be charged by way of cash against proper receipt or by demand draft or bankers cheque payable to the Accounts officer of the public Authority at the following rates:

   a) for information provided in diskette or floppy – Rs. 50/- per diskette or floppy; and

   b) for information provided in printed form at the price fixed for such publication or Rs. two per page of photocopy for extracts from the publication.

Sd/-
(Hari Kumar)
Director

[F.No. 34012/8(s)/2005-Estt.(B)]

To
The Manager,
Government of India Press,
Mayapuri, New Delhi.
No. 34012/8(s)/2005-Estt.(B) New Delhi, dated the 16th September, 2005

Copy to:-
1. All Ministries / Departments of the Government of India
2. Comptroller & Auditor General of India, New Delhi
3. Union Public Service Commission, New Delhi
4. Central Vigilance Commission, New Delhi
5. Central Bureau of Investigation, New Delhi
6. Chief Secretaries of State Governments and Union Territory Administrations
7. Lok Sabha / Rajya Sabha Secretariat
8. All attached and subordinate offices of the Ministry of Personnel,
Public Grievances and Pensions and Ministry of Home Affairs
9. All Officers and sections of the Ministry of Personnel, Public Grievances and Pensions and Ministry of Home Affairs.

Sd/-
(Hari Kumar)
Director

(TO BE PUBLISHED IN PART-II, SECTION 3, SUB-SECTION (i)
OF THE GAZETTE OF INDIA, EXTRA-ORDINARY
DATED THE 27TH OCTOBER,2005)

Government of India
Ministry of Personnel, Public Grievances and Pensions
(Department of Personnel and Training)

New Delhi, dated the 27th October, 2005

Notification

G.S.R……..(E)._ In exercise of the powers conferred by clauses (b) and (c) of sub-section (2) of section 27 of the Right to Information Act, 2005 (22 of 2005), the Central Government hereby makes the following rules to amend the Right to Information (Regulation of Fee and Cost) Rules, 2005, namely :-

1. Short title and commencement – (1) These rules may be called the Right to Information (Regulation of Fee and Cost) (Amendment) Rules, 2005.

(2) They shall come into force on the date of their publication in the Official Gazette.

2. In the Right to Information (Regulation of Fee and Cost) Rules, 2005, in rule 4, for clause (d), the following clause shall be substituted, namely-

"(d) for inspection of records, no fee for the first hour; and a fee of rupees five for each subsequent hour (or fraction thereof)."

[F.No. 34012/8(s)/2005-Estt. (B)]

(T.Jacob)
Joint Secretary to the Government of India

Note: The Principal rules were published in the Gazette of India vide Ministry of Personnel, Public Grievances and Pensions (Department of Personnel and Training) notification No. 34012/8(s)/2005-Estt. (B) dated 16th September, 2005 [G.S.R. No. 336 dated 1st October, 2005, Part II, section 3, sub-section (i)]

(T.Jacob)
Joint Secretary to the Government of India

To
The Manager,
Government of India Press,
Mayapuri, New Delhi.

[TO BE PUBLISHED IN PART II, SECTION 3, SUB-SECTION (I)
OF THE GAZETTE OF INDIA, EXTRA-ORDINARY
DATED THE 28TH OCTOBER, 2005]

Government of India
Ministry of Personnel, Public Grievances and Pensions
(Department of Personnel and Training)

New Delhi dated 28th October, 2005

Notification

GSR.....(E)._ In exercise of the powers conferred by clauses (e) and (f) of sub-section (2) of section 27of the Right to Information Act, 2005 (22 of 2005), the Central Government hereby makes the following rules, namely:-

1. Short title and commencement.- (1) These rules may be called the Central Information Commission (Appeal Procedure) Rules, 2005.

(2) They shall come into force on the date of their publication in the Official Gazette.

2. Definitions- In these rules, unless the context otherwise requires,-
   - (a) "Act" means the Right to Information Act, 2005;
   - (b) "section" means section of the Act;
   - (c) "Commission" means the Central Information Commission;
   - (d) words and expressions used herein and not defined but defined in the Act, shall have the

meanings respectively assigned to them in that Act.

3. Contents of appeal:- An appeal to the Commission shall contain the following information, namely :-

(i) name and address of the appellant;

(ii) name and address of the Central Public Information Officer against the decision of whom the appeal is preferred;

(iii) particulars of the order including number, if any, against which the appeal is preferred;

(iv) brief facts leading to the appeal

(v) if the appeal is preferred against deemed refusal, the particulars of the application, including number and date and name and address of the Central Public Information Officer to whom the application was made;

(vi) prayer or relief sought;

(vii) grounds for the prayer or relief;

(viii) verification by the appellant; and

(ix) any other information which the Commission may deem necessary for deciding the appeal.

4. Documents to accompany appeal.- Every appeal made to the Commission shall be accompanied by the following documents, namely :-

(i) self-attested copies of the Orders or documents against which the appeal is being preferred;

(ii) copies of documents relied upon by the appellant and referred to in the appeal; and

(iii) an index of the documents referred to in the appeal.

5. Procedure in deciding appeal.- In deciding the appeal the Commission may,-

(i) hear oral or written evidence on oath or on affidavit from concerned or interested person;

(ii) peruse or inspect documents, public records or copies thereof;

(iii) inquire through authorised officer further details or facts;

(iv) hear Central Public Information Officer, Central Assistant Public Information Officer or such Senior Officer who decide the first appeal, or such person against whom the complaint is made, as the case may be;

(v) hear third party; and

(vi) receive evidence on affidavits from Central Public Information Officer, Central Assistant Public Information Officer, such Senior Officer who decided the first appeal, such person against whom the complaint lies or the third party.

6. Service of notice by Commission.- Notice to be issued by the Commission may be served in any of the following modes, namely :-

(i) service by the party itself;

(ii) by hand delivery (dasti) through Process Server;

(iii) by registered post with acknowledgement due; or

(iv) through Head of office or Department.

7. Personal presence of the appellant or complainant.-

(1) The appellant or the complainant, as the case may be, shall in every case be informed of the date of hearing at least seven clear days before that date.

(2) The appellant or the complainant, as the case may be, may at his discretion at the time of hearing of the appeal or complaint by the Commission be present in person or through his duly authorised representative or may opt not to be present.

(3) Where the Commission is satisfied that the circumstances exist due to which the appellant or the complainant, as the case may be, is being prevented from attending the hearing of the Commission, then, the Commission may afford the appellant or the complainant, as the case may be, another opportunity of being heard before a final decision is taken or take any other appropriate action as it may deem fit.

(4) The appellant or the complainant, as the case may be, may seek the assistance of any person in the process of the appeal while presenting his points and the person representing him may not be a legal practitioner.

8. Order of the Commission.- Order of the Commission shall be pronounced in open proceedings and be in writing duly authenticated by the Registrar or any other officer authorised by the Commission for this purpose.

[F.No. 1/4/2005-IR]

(T.Jacob)
Joint Secretary to the Government of India

To

The Manager,

Government of India Press,

Mayapuri, New Delhi.

No. 1/4/2005-IR New Delhi, dated the 28th October, 2005.

Copy to :

1. All Ministries/Departments of the Government of India.
2. Comptroller and Auditor General of India, New Delhi.
3. Union Public Service Commission, New Delhi.
4. Central Vigilance Commission, New Delhi.
5. Central Bureau of Investigation, New Delhi.
6. Chief Secretaries of State Governments and Union Territory Administrations.
7. Lok Sabha/Rajya Sabha Secretariat.
8. All Attached and Subordinate Offices of the Ministry of Personnel, Public Grievances and Pensions and Ministry of Home Affairs.
9. All Officers and Sections of the Ministry of Personnel, Public Grievances and Pensions and Ministry of Home Affairs.

(Hari Kumar)

Director

Annexure 3

Before the Central Information Commission

Second Appeal under Section 19(3) of the Right to Information Act, 2005

Sample format for drafting Second Appeals

S.No.	Particulars Required	
1.	Names and Address of the Appellant	To be filled up by the Appellant
2(I)	a) Name and Address of the Central Public Information Officer against the Decision of whom the appeal if preferred (b) Date of Application (c) Date of Reply from PIO/CPIO	Try to provide the information as required in this Template column(s)
(II)	(a) Name and Address of Frist Apellate Authority (b) Date of First Appeal (c) Date of Order of First Appellate Authority	

3	Particulars of the order including order number, if any, against which the appeal is preferred:	
4	Brief facts leading to the appeal	
5	If the appeal is preferred against deemed refusal, the particulars of the application, including numberand date, name and address of the Central Public Information Officer to whom the application was made	
6	Prayers or Relief Sought	
7	Grounds for Prayer or Relief	
8	Verification by the Appellant	
9	Any other information which the Commission may deem necessary for deciding the appeal	

Note: Please submit four copies of your second appeal to the Commission.

Annexure 4

Chief Information Commissioner of India

Shri Wajahat Habibullah
Chief Information Commissioner
Central Information Commission
Block IV, 5th Floor,
Old JNU Campus.
New Delhi- 110 067
Tel: 011- 26717355 (o)
Email:whabibullah@nic.in
Website: www.cic.gov.in

Chief Information Commissioners of States

S.N.	Name of Chief Information Commissioner	State / UT	Contact
1	2	3	4
1	Shri. C.D. Arha	Andhra Pradesh	2nd Floor, Haka Bhavan (Near Vidhan Sabha) Hyderabad - 500022 Tel: 040-2345620/55405566
2	Shri. Nyodek Yongan	Arunachal Pradesh	Arunachal Pradesh Information Commission Govt. of Arunachal Pradesh Itanagar - 791111
3	Shri. R.S. Mushahary	Assam	Guwahati, DispurJunta Bhavan Guwahati Tel: 0361-2262704 (O) Email: scic-as@nic.in
4	Shri G. Madhavan	Chandigarh	SCO No. 70-71 Scetor 8-C Chandigarh Tel: 0172-2726568 Fax: 0172-2783834 E-mail: madhavang@hry.nic.in Website: www.cicharyana.gov.in

5	Shri.A.K. VijayVargia	Chhattisgarh	Nirmal Chayya Bhawan Mira Dattar Road, Near Bottle House Shankar Nagar, Raipur - 492 007 Tel: 0771-2221259, 4080013 Fax: 0771-2221204 Email: akvijayvariga@nic.in
6	Shri. A Venkatratnam	Goa	Shrama Shakthi Bhavan, Ground Floor, Patto Panaji, Goa - 403 401 Tel: 0832-2413774 (O)
7	Dr. P.K. Das	Gujarat	1st Floor, Bureau of Economics & Statistics Building, Sector-18, Gandhinagar - 382018, Tel: Office: 079-23252701 Secretary: 079-23252966 Email: gscic@gujarat.gov.in
8	Shri. G Madhavan	Harayana	SCO No. 70-71 Sector 8C, Madhya Marg, Chandigarh Tel: 0172-2726568 Email: madhavang@hry.nic.in Website: www.cicharyana.gov.in
9	Shri P.S. Rana	Himachal Pradesh	Room No.222, Armsdale Building HP Secretariat Shimla-171 002 Tel: 0177-2621904 / 2880726
10	Shri Sunderlal Singh	Manipur	Old Secretariat, Imphal - 795001 Tel: 0385-2220981 Fax: 0385-2220981 E-mail: sunderlal@nic.in

1	2	3	4
11	Shri. Harishankar Pradesh	Jharkhand	Engineer's Hostel, (Next to Canara Bank) Sector III, Post-Dhurwa Ranchi - 834004 Mobile: 09431364947
12	Shri. K K Misra	Karnataka	3rd floor, 3rd Stage, Multistoried Buildings Dr.Ambedkar Road, Bangalore - 560 001 Tel: 080-22371191 Email: scic@karnataka.gov.in Website: http://www.kic.gov.in
13	Shri. Palatt Mohandas	Kerala	Punnen Road Thiruvananthapuram - 695039 Tel: 0471-2320920 Fax: 0471-2330920
14	Shri. T N Shrivastava	Madhya Pradesh	Nirwachan Bhawan, Second Floor, 58, Arera Hills, Bhopal - 462 011 Tel: 0755-2761367 Website: http://www.mpsic.nic.in
15	Shri. Suresh Vinayakrao Joshi	Maharashtra	15th Floor, New Administrative Building Madame Cama Road, Opposite Mantralaya Mumbai - 400 0032 Tel: 022-22856078
16	Shri. G P Wahlang	Meghalaya	Meghalaya Secretariat, Shillong – 1 Tel: 064-2226102 Email: gpw@shillong.meg.nic.in

17	Shri. Robert Hrangdawla	Mizoram	Tel: 0389-2334833 (O); 0389-2316001(R); Mobile: 09436140247
18	Shri. P. Takutenheb Ao	Nagaland	Old Secretariat Complex Post Box 148, Kohima - 79701 Tel: 0370-2291595 Fax: 0370-2291774 Mobile: 09436140247
19	Shri. Dhirendra Nath Padhi	Orissa	Orissa Soochna Commission, (Secretary), State Guest House Annexe, Room No. 44, Unit 5, Bhubaneshwar - 751001 Tel: 0674-2534300 Email: hon_scic@ori.nic.in Website: http://orissasoochanacommission.nic.in
20	Shri C.S. Khairwal	Puducherry	Chief Secretariat, C Block, 3rd Floor Beach Road, Puducherry - 605001 Tel: 0413-2233327 Fax: 0413-23337575 E-mail: cs@pon.nic.in
21	Shri. Rajan Kashyap	Punjab	131 Sector-10, Chandigarh - 160011 Tel: 0172-2740543 (O) 0172-2740353 (R) Fax: 0172-2740543 Website: http://www.infocommpunjab.com
22	Shri. M. D. Kaurani	Rajasthan	Yojana Bhavan, 2nd Floor, Tilak Marg, C-Scheme, Jaipur - 303005 Tel: 0141-2220299 / 2222011

1	2	3	4
23	Shri D.K. Gazmer	Sikkim	Tashiling Secretariat Gangtok - 737101 Tel: 09434023532
24	Shri. S Ramakrishnan	Tamilnadu	No.89, Dr Alagappa Road Purasaiwalkam Chennai 600084 Website: http://www.tn.gov.in/rti/sic.htm
25	Shri. B K Chakraborty	Tripura	Civil Secretariat, Agartala, West Tripura - 799001 Tel: 0381-2218021 Email: scic-tic-tr@nic.in
26	Shri. R S Tolia	Uttaranchal	4 Subhash Road, 4th Floor, Dehradun - 248001 Tel: 0135-2712100; 2712200; 2712079 Fax: 0135 - 2666779
27	Justice Mohd Asgar Khan	Uttar Pradesh	Uttar Pradesh State Information Commission 6th Floor, Indira Bhavan, Lucknow - 751001 Tel: 0522-2288599; 2288598
28	Shri.Arun Bhattacharya	West Bengal	Writers Building Kolkata-700001 Tel: 033 - 22215858

Annexure 5

Useful Links, NGOs

List of websites on Right to Information

- www.righttoinformation.info
- www.parivartan.com
- www.righttoinformation.org
- www.kabir.org.in
- www.snsindia.org
- www.rti.gov.in
- www.righttoinformation.gov.in
- www.humanrightsinitiative.org
- www.persmin.nic.in
- www.rtiindia.org
- rti-india.pbwiki.com
- www.indiahowto.com/how-to-save-india-from-corruption.html
- www.rti.aidindia.org
- en.wikipedia.org/wiki/Right_to_Information_Act
- www.answers.com/topic/right-to-information-act
- http://ww1.transparency.org/
- www.foi-asia.org/
- www.samarthan.org/
- http://syg.com/web/mstrust/manju/scmadmin/Home.php
- http://www.pria.org/rti.htm

E-discussion Groups on Right to Information

- Hum Janenge: HumJanenge-subscribe@yahoogroups.co.in
- Anti Bribery: antibriberycampaign-subscribe@ yahoogroups.com
- RTI India: rti_india-subscribe@yahoogroups.com
- IndiaRTI: INDIARTI-subscribe@yahoogroups.com

Blogs on Right to Information

- http://indiarti.blogspot.com
- http://right2information.wordpress.com/tag/rti-blogs/

List and contact details of some of the organizations working in the area of Right to Information

1. Society for Andaman and Nicobar Ecology (Andaman and Nicobar)
   c/o Tarang Traders, Port Blair, A&N Islands
   Tel: 03192-232929; 234624
   Email:sane@andamanisles.com; samiracharya.sane@gmail.com

2. Centre for Good Governance (Andhra Pradesh)
Dr. MCR HRD IAP Campus,
Road No. 25, Jubilee Hills,
Hyderabad 500033
Andhra Pradesh (India).
Email : info@cgg.gov.in

3. North East Network (Assam)
Jorpukhuri, JN Borooah lane,
Guwahati, Assam -781001
Tel: 0361-2603833
Email: assamnen@yahoo.co.uk

4. Consumer Rights Education and Awareness Trust (CREAT) (Karnataka)
239, 5th C Main, Remco Layout,
Vijayanagar, Bangalore-560040
Tel: 080 – 23357280
Email: creatorg@sify.com

5. Meghalaya Right to Information Movement (Megahalaya)
C/o Dr. M.S. Dunn
Laban, Shillong, Meghalaya - 793004
Email: meghalayarti@gmail.com

6. SAMARTHAN-Center For Development Support (Madhya Pradesh)
36, Green Avenue Chuna Bhatti
Bhopal (M.P) 462016
Tel: 91-755-2467625,2420918
Fax: 91-755-2468663
Email: y_kumar003@yahoo.co.in;

samarthan@samarthan.org

7. SCOPE (Jammu & Kashmir)
7 Panj Bakhtar Road, Jammu-Tawi
Tel: 0191-2548534
E-mail: scope@scopeforchange.org

8. Satark Nagrik Sangathan (New Delhi)
B-76 (Garage) S.F.S. Flats
Sheikh Sarai-1
New Delhi-110017
Tel: 011- 26011362, 09811420295

9. Parivartan (New Delhi)
3/57, Sundernagri,
Near St. Stephen's Dispensary
Delhi-100 093
Tel: 011-65254077
Email: parivartan_india@rediffmail.com

10. Commonwealth Human Rights Initiative (CHRI) (New Delhi)
B-117, Second Floor, Sarvodaya Enclave
New Delhi - 110 017
Tel: 011- 26850523, 26528152, 26864678
Fax: 011-26864688
E-mail: chriall@nda.vsnl.net.in

11. KABIR (New Delhi)
E 109, Pandav Nagar, Delhi- 100 092
Tel: 011- 22485139
Email: kabir.rti@gmail.com

12. JOSH (New Delhi)
405F, Pocket II,

Mayur Vihar Phase – I
New Delhi - 110091
Tel: 011- 43042669
Website: http://josh4india.org

13. National Campaign for People's Right to Information (NCPRI) (New Delhi)
14, Tower 2, Supreme Enclave,
Mayur Vihar- Phase - I
Delhi - 110 091
Tel: 022- 32903776 (Mumbai)
Email: ncpri.india@gmail.com

14. PRIA (New Delhi)
42, Tuglakabad Institutional Area,
New Delhi – 110062
Tel: 011- 29956908, 29960931/32/33
Email:info@pria.org

15. Mazdoor Kisan Shakti Sangathan (MKSS) (Rajasthan)
Village Devdungri, Post- Barar,
District Rajasmand- 313341
Tel: 02951- 243254, 250180
Email: mkssrajasthan@gmail.com

16. JANPATH (Gujarat)
B-3, Sahajanand Towers, Jivaraj Park,
Vejalpur road,
Ahmedabad 380051, Gujarat
Tel: 079-682 1553, 6820719, 6821190, 09824048842
Email: janpath1ad1@rediffmail.com,
janpath1ad1@wilnetonline.net

National Campaign for People's Right to Information (NCPRI)

The National Campaign for People's Right to Information (NCPRI), launched in 1996, seeks to empower the people and to deepen democracy, through promoting people's right to information. Through the use of this right, it seeks to fight corruption and social apathy, to make governments, and other institutions and agencies having an impact on public welfare, more humane and accountable to the people, and to promote efficiency and frugality. The NCPRI is committed to support participatory, just, secular and humane democracy.

The NCPRI endeavours to constantly engage and interact with the state and with other institutions and agencies. It campaigns for the enactment and use of a right to information law that is effective and accessible to all, and supports people's efforts at developing the ability and motivation to use the right to information for addressing individual and social problems. It works at disseminating the RTI law and encourages and supports the development of materials related to transparency and governance, the raising of awareness about the fundamental value of information, the conduct of research, and the setting up of information clearing houses. It seeks to further the cause of transparency by adopting other direct and indirect methods, including the filing of information requests, the fighting of legal cases, and the holding of public hearings.

The NCPRI seeks to actively work with other progressive campaigns and movements and in solidarity with other progressive elements of society.

Contact details:

National Campaign for People's Right to Information (NCPRI)
ncpri.india@gmail.com
www.righttoinformation.info

Printed: Pushpak Press Pvt.Ltd. 203-204, Okhla Industrial Area, Phase-I, New Delhi-110020